Copyright
Williams Ph.D.

All rights reserved. No part of this publication may be reproduced, distributed, or transmitted in any form or by any means, including photocopying, recording, or other electronic or mechanical methods, without the prior written permission of the publisher, except in the case of brief quotation embodied in critical reviews and certain other noncommercial uses permitted by copyright law.

Contents

INTRODUCTION 4
   A Brief History Of Breeding 6
How To Breed Dogs 13
   Choosing Which of Your Dogs to Breed 20
   Examining Your Dogs 25
   Starting the Breeding Process 28
   Dealing With the Delivery 34
   Taking Care of the Puppies 38
How Much Does Dog Breeding Cost? 42
   Dog Breeding For Beginners – Pros & Cons 45
Guide to Responsible Dog Breeding 52
      MATING 74
   Pregnancy and Whelping Preparation 79
      Keep Your Puppies Warm, Fed and Clean 91
      Commit Yourself to the Puppies for Life 107
      Encourage New Owners to Register Their Puppy 109
   Dog Breeding How To's 119
   DOG BREEDING – HOW TO FIND A DOG MATE 128
   DOG BREEDING – THINGS TO THINK ABOUT 134
   THREE REASONS WHY YOU SHOULD NOT BREED YOUR DOG! 140
   DOG BREEDING AND HEREDITARY EYE PROBLEMS 144
   THE IMPORTANCE OF MEDICAL CHECKS 150

Do you have the resources to breed successfully?............. 156
Choosing a stud.. 160
CONCLUSION 162

INTRODUCTION

Dog breeding is a purposeful bringing together of a stud and a bitch during the fertile portion of the bitch's heat cycle in order for the animals to mate and produce a litter. No breeding should ever be undertaken lightly. There are thousands, if not millions, of unwanted pets in need of a stable and loving home, so any breeding should be given ample consideration before deciding to proceed. Getting involved in dog breeding should be undertaken seriously and with a focus on learning all the ins and outs related to the basics of dog breeding. This includes genetics, health testing, the estrus and gestation cycles, whelping puppies and caring for the newborn puppies. Breeding a dog and continuing on the traditions of your favorite breed can be immensely rewarding, but a responsible breeder will do all of their homework first to make sure their efforts are successful.

A Brief History Of Breeding

A Golden Retriever greets his boy after school, a tennis ball in his mouth, ready for a game of fetch. An English Springer Spaniel leaps forward to bring back a fallen bird. A Pomeranian snuggles with his owner, who's laid up with a broken back. A Doberman Pinscher accompanies his owner as she jogs through the park at night.

For as long as we've known them— 15,000 years or more—dogs have been our assistants, hunting buddies, protectors, and friends. How did a single species develop so many talents? Why have dogs, more than any other species, become our partners in almost any endeavor?

The answer lies not only in their plasticity—the range of sizes and shapes they come in—but also in human creativity. Dogs are designer animals, cut from the fabric of our needs and fashioned to suit almost any purpose.

Early dog pleased early man

In the beginning, dogs barked an alarm when wild animals or strangers approached the outskirts of the human settlements where they lived, scavenging meals from the communal garbage dump. They kept down vermin by ridding the area of rotting food. Dog's first job, then, was to act as a combination security and waste management system. Since both services were valued by early humans, their presence was tolerated.

We don't know how dogs made their way from the farthest edges of village life to the greater warmth and comfort of the Mesolithic hearth, but move they did. Although early people didn't know anything about genetics or heritable traits, they probably kept the puppies with the loudest and most insistent barks, the better to alert them to predators.

Breeding becomes a hobby

Breeding as we know it today is a fairly recent invention. For the most part, it wasn't until the 19th century that people began to keep records of canine bloodlines and to classify dogs into specific breeds rather than generic types such as hunting dog, hound, herding dog, or lap dog. Breeders ranged from noblemen creating a better retriever to shepherds refining herding ability for their particular livestock.

Today, we live with more than 400 dog breeds recognized by kennel clubs around the world, which govern dog shows, field trials, hunt tests, herding tests, and other measures of quality and working ability. While many of those dogs still perform the work for which they've been bred for centuries or even millennia, the majority of them live with us as companions, perhaps the most important job of all.

Plenty of variety within a breed

Choosing a purebred is the best way to know what you're getting in a dog as far as looks and temperament, although it's never an ironclad guarantee. Each breed is known for a particular temperament, but even within breeds we find variety. The Rottweiler can be clownish or commonsensical, the Papillon intensely energetic or lovingly laidback, the Greyhound friendly or retiring.

Those differences can be related to how frequently he was handled as a very young puppy, how well you socialized and trained him after you brought him home, as well as the genetic luck of the draw.

Your dog will be as individual as you are, a radical notion to some people, but one that's essential to the success of your relationship. If you accept it, you're sure to be rewarded.

Whatever dog you choose, and wherever you acquire him—reputable breeder, animal shelter, or breed rescue group, the two of you will be a new link in a chain of friendship stretching back thousands of years.

How To Breed Dogs

Breeding dogs can be a very fulfilling and exciting task as long as you understand the responsibilities and risks involved in the process. While having a bunch of puppies running around seems adorable and fun, they also require a lot of work and attention! If you're interesting in breeding dogs, you need to make sure you're prepared for the job.

Deciding to Breed

Do your research. Before you can decide if you are ready and fit to breed, you need to do research. This will help you know what the process means and what you will have to do. Read books by reputable breeders or veterinarians. Talk to your veterinarian about the pros and cons. Talk to other reputable breeders about the realities of breeding.

Have the right reasons. The only responsible reason to breed is based on previous experience and research. If you have spent the last two or more years training, working and competing your dog, you are a good candidate for breeding dogs. Bringing high quality, healthy puppies into the world requires work and research.

You shouldn't breed dogs to sell them as pets. This is not a profitable or responsible way to breed. This reason creates a market, which unfortunately drives the many puppy farms found across the United States. Please be responsible and do not be someone who contributes to the pet overpopulation problem.

Breeding dogs properly and responsibly takes a lot of time and investment.

Examine your situation. Make sure you determine that you have an exceptional example of your breed. You do so with the help of experts. You want to improve the breed, so you need to have evidence that your dog is within the top 10% of the specific breed. You want your dog to contribute positively to the genetic pool.

Your dog should be healthy and talented. Your dog should also have a symmetrical physical appearance that matches up to the breed standards. Your dog should also have an exceptional temperament.

You need to be prepared to live with the puppies for a minimum of 8 weeks before they leave your house for new homes. You need to know what time of the year the breeding may happen. This can help you figure out how it will affect you and your family.

Be prepared to keep all the puppies. You are responsible for their health and happiness. If for some reason you cannot get them all homes, you may have to keep them all.

Learn what dogs are good to breed. There are a few types of dogs that are good candidates for breeding. There are also hereditary traits that can be valuable to pass down to new puppies as well. You can breed working dogs. Their talents are based on the dog's ability to retrieve and herd livestock or track prey. You can also breed show dogs, which are judged based on their physical appearance and behavior.

In working dogs, the tendency for a dog to be good at those jobs can be hereditary. The dam and sire dogs need to have proven track records out in the field. There are competitions to prove a dog is able to perform.

Your show dogs need to follow conformation. This is the standard of physical appearance for every dog breed. Every breed has a breed standard set by the American Kennel Club for the United States. Dogs bred to meet these standards are judged in a show ring against others to determine which dog best represents the breed's standards.

Other countries have their own breeding standards. If you plan to show is other countries, look for the conformation standards in the area.

Choosing Which of Your Dogs to Breed

Choose your dog. You need to choose which of your dogs you are going to breed. You need to choose a dam, which is a female dog capable of having puppies. You also need a stud, which is a male dog you want to breed with a dam. You need to make sure they have the discussed characteristics.

You can also get a stud from a different breeder if you don't have one.

Hiring a stud or purchasing semen costs money. Sometimes the arrangement allows the owner of the sire pick of the litter. Make sure that all agreements are written and signed so that there is a contract between all parties involved with the litter.

Determine their genetics. You should look into the dogs' genetic backgrounds. Examine the bloodline of your dogs to make sure they have good qualities in their bloodline. For purebred dogs, you can obtain their bloodlines from the American Kennel Club or other registering authority. You must also ensure the pair are not directly related to prevent genetic defects of inbreeding.

You should have your dog and the dog you want to breed them with tested for genetic problems associated with their breed. The Orthopedic Foundation of America (OFA) manages a database of dogs and their test results for genetic problems like hip and elbow dysplasia, eye conditions, patellar luxation, and heart problems. You do not want to breed dogs with health conditions that can be passed on to the next generation.

Observe their temperament. Watch the dogs you want to breed to examine their behavior. This should be with each other as well as other dogs. Breeding friendly, well balanced dogs tends to increase the chances of the puppies having similar temperaments. Aggressive and overly fearful dogs should not be bred. They are dangerous.

Check the dogs' ages. You need to be sure that your dogs are breeding age. Most dogs need to around 2 years old. Many genetic issues will show up by 24 months of age. You can have these screened in specific tests. For example, the OFA will not accept the x-rays of dogs until 24 months for hip dysplasia evaluation and grading. To breed successfully, your dogs will need permanent identification in the form of a microchip or a tattoo to be able to submit testing data for evaluation by the OFA and other entities. They want to make sure there is no way to falsify the results.

Dams begin their heats, or estrus cycles, between 6 and 9 months. They go into heat every 5-11 months after their first cycle. Most breeders do not breed a dam until she is 2 years old and has had 3 or 4 cycles. This is the point where she is fully mature. She is also physically able to endure the stress of carrying and delivering pups.

Examining Your Dogs

Take your dogs to the vet. Before you breed your dog, you need to have the dog checked by your veterinarian. Make sure that your dog is up to date on vaccinations. Her antibodies will be passed on to the puppies through her milk. These antibodies protect the puppies from getting sick.

Know your dog's medical history. If your dog has unknown medical problems, it can change your breeding plans. Small breed dogs can have genetic conditions that you want to understand before breeding. The puppies are likely to have the same problems, or worse. Issues can include dental problems such as malocclusions, a condition where the upper and lower jaws do not meet together properly. They can be prone to dislocation in their knee caps, hip or elbow dysplasia, and spine problems such as disc rupture. They may also have allergies leading to skin and ear infections, heart conditions, eye problems, or behavior problems.

Make sure that your dog is on a deworming program. Roundworms, Hookworms and Heart worms can be passed from the mom dog to the puppies.

Have a breeding soundness exam. You need to have your animals checked to make sure they are able to breed. This may include a semen analysis for your male dog. For example, these tests can find genetic problems as well as contagious diseases like Brucellosis. Before breeding a sire or dam, Brucellosis testing is recommended to make sure neither dog is a carrier and could pass it on to the other.

Starting the Breeding Process

Wait for the dam to go into heat. Your dam needs to be in heat before she can be bred. The timing is not set in stone, so watch you dam to know when this happens. The dam's genital area will begin to swell and there may be a bloody discharge. If you have the stud in a nearby pen, he will get more excited and interested in the female.

The dam will not accept the stud until she is ready to breed. She may even snap at him to keep him away until she is ready. Do not let your dogs get injured. Monitor them closely when they are together.

Typically, the female will be receptive about 9-11 days into the heat cycle and allow the sire to mount and mate her.

If you have difficulty getting your dam bred, your veterinarian can do Progesterone testing. This helps find out when she is in estrus and her body is ready to accept semen. Progesterone levels will rise 1-2 days before ovulation. Some dams will have silent heat cycles which make estrus difficult to detect and Progesterone testing will help pin down ovulation timing.

Consider artificial insemination. Artificial insemination can help you breed your dog if you don't have a stud. Frozen dog semen can be shipped around the world stored in liquid nitrogen. Specific steps are taken to thaw it and inseminate the female dog. You may need to consider this if the pair you chose cannot seem to breed naturally.

This can be problematic because It raises questions about the potential problems for the next generation's breeding soundness.

In really special cases, semen can be surgically implanted into the uterus by a veterinarian with the dam under anesthesia. Of course, these extra procedures increase the cost of each pregnancy and each puppy in the litter.

Keep your dam healthy. When you are sure the dam has been bred, you can separate her from the stud. You need to feed her a balanced diet. You can also give her supplemental vitamins, such as calcium. These are typically recommended by your vet.

This needs to happen over the course of the pregnancy. The gestation period for dogs is 58-68 days.

Keep the dam's kennel free of infestations such as fleas. Clean it regularly and provide lots of fresh water and clean bedding.

Notice changes to your dam. The nipples and mammary glands undergo changes during pregnancy. Toward the end of pregnancy, the mammary glands will start to fill with milk. During the last three weeks of her pregnancy, she will require extra nutrition. Discuss proper nutrition with your veterinarian.

Typically, the pregnant female is fed puppy food during the last three weeks of pregnancy. This provides her with adequate calories and nutrition for the growing fetuses and helps prepare her for lactation.

Dealing With the Delivery

Prepare a whelping box. A whelping box is what will be used to deliver the puppies. This box should be about 6 inches (15.2 cm) longer than the female when she is lying prone, and a foot or so wider. It should have a rail to prevent her from laying on the pups after they are born.

Place alternating layers of plastic sheeting and newspapers in the bottom of the box. This helps keep it cleaner when the bottom becomes soiled. You can just slide out a layer of paper and a sheet of plastic, leaving a clean one in its place. Include clean towels or other bedding that can be easily laundered.

Be alert. You need to be aware of when the time for delivery is near. Educate yourself on the stages of labor. Once she starts delivering puppies, monitor her for strong contractions longer than 30-45 minutes that do not produce a puppy. This may signal complications during the delivery.

Having x-rays done at 45 days of gestation will allow your veterinarian to count how many fetal skeletons are present. This also shows if there are any abnormally large puppies inside that may cause problems delivering. This information will prepare you and your veterinarian for the possibility of a c-section and give you an idea of how many puppies to expect.

Keep the pups warm. When the puppies are born, you need to keep them warm. You also need to make sure they are all able to nurse. Examine them for birth defects like a cleft palate. The roof of a puppy's mouth should be complete, with no evidence of a separation of the oral tissue. The dam will clean the pups and help the puppies get into position to nurse.

If there is a cleft palate, milk will go from the mouth into the nasal passages. If it is a severe enough situation, the puppy should be euthanized because they will not survive.

Record the birth. Write down the birth date, total number of pups, and the number of each sex. If you are planning on registering the litter with organizations such as the AKC, you can do so online. You will need the registration numbers of the dam and sire when filling out the form.

Taking Care of the Puppies

Monitor the puppies. Watch the puppies carefully the first few weeks, making sure they stay clean and warm. Also make sure they are getting enough milk. Weigh the puppies on a gram scale daily to ensure that they are gaining weight. Healthy puppies should be absolutely clean, active, and have full bellies. Puppies should gain about 10% of their body weight per day for the first 2 weeks of life.

At about 4 weeks, they will begin to get very active. The whelping box will no longer be large enough. Give them a larger, safe enclosure to explore. The dam will likely leave them alone for longer periods of time. You can start weaning the puppies on to soaked puppy kibble at this time.

Take them to the vet. Take the puppies to the vet when they are 7 to 8 weeks old. The veterinarian will give them their first vaccinations. These include Distemper, Hepatitis, Parvo, and

Para influenza or DHPP. They are also treated for worms. Flea and heartworm prevention should be discussed.

Have your veterinarian check for other health or hereditary problems as well. A responsible breeder will provide this information to the new owners of the puppies so that the new family can properly complete the puppy's vaccination series during the recommended time frame.

Screen new puppy owners. This process needs to be done carefully. You want to make sure that you are sending the puppy to a great home. The new family should be responsible and prepared to devote time, energy, and resources to the new dog.

Consider a home inspection. Be prepared to turn down a family if they are not a good fit for one of your puppies.

Create a contract. When you find the right puppy owners, you should draw up a contract with them. Make sure to include any health guarantees that you are providing and what the limitations of those may be. Include that the family must return the puppy to you should they be unable to keep it for any time during the pet's life.

You should also Indicate whether the puppy was sold as a pet or a breeding prospect and if there are any requirements for spaying/neutering by a specific age.

How Much Does Dog Breeding Cost?

Purchasing a female dog is the very first cost that you incur. Pick the right breed and make sure that it's popular. However, those that have female dogs will have other concerns to attend to. For purchasing a female dog, it can already cost you around $800. In order to breed effectively, the female dog needs to undergo a series of tests like hip x-rays, thyroid tests, and eye tests. By doing so, the vet can identify if your female dog has dysplasia, cataracts, and other diseases.

These different tests can reach as high as $300. Responsible owners will see to it that the tests are completed to ensure the health of the puppies. However, some female dog owners still opt not to have their dogs checked because they claim that they can't afford to pay for such expenses.

Female dogs should be at the right age (2 years and older) before you can subject them to breeding. During the early years, you will spend about $1,000 for the vitamins, toys, and food of your pet. Minimum stud fees range from $400 to a few hundred dollars more. Routines exams are required once the dog is pregnant. That will cost you another $500 or so.

Can you still consider dog breeding as an affordable venture? Try to think about it. If money is not a problem, you can proceed. Special equipments are also needed like hemostats, towels, tweezers, baby scales, suction bulbs, and many others. Decide now and see how things work for you.

Dog Breeding For Beginners – Pros & Cons

In every activity, there will always be pros and cons. This is also true with dog breeding. As the breeder, you need to weigh these things before you finally set out to breed dogs.

If you think that dog breeding is inexpensive, you're very wrong. It involves a lot of responsibilities and tasks that you need to carry out without delay. Health considerations are also vital and this should be closely observed both in the female and male dogs. The final decision should only be made after careful thinking and discussion with family members and of course, your vet.

Pros

Here are the pros or positives in breeding a female dog. It's really rewarding to be able to produce the best-standard puppies. The feeling is also different once you find a suitable home for the pups. Make sure that you choose only the loving and caring individuals so that your puppies won't end up in animal shelters.

You may be able to develop championship lines of dogs. The kennel will have increased awareness if one of your pups is proclaimed champion.

Cons

As a breeder, you need to be aware that different dog breeds have different unique characteristics and issues. As a breeder, there are certain negatives or drawbacks that you may encounter.

Stud services are quite costly especially the popular and experienced ones. If you want to opt for the championship bloodline, you will need to spend hundred to thousands in order to access a purebred male.

The female dog is weaker than the male and so she is more prone to health risks. Some female dogs get injured during mating while others develop certain conditions which can threaten the life of your bitch. When left unsupervised, your dog may die while giving birth to the puppies. It requires a lot of your attention which is inconvenient on your part especially if you have other things to attend to.

Once the female is impregnated, you will incur additional vet expenses because the female needs to be checked regularly. You will also pay for the vaccinations, shots, and other vet costs. It can reach thousands of dollars depending on how frequent you visit the vet's clinic.

There will always be health issues concerning the puppies. If you want, you can make arrangements with the owner of the stud just in case health problems arise after the birth of the pups. Besides, problems or faults are usually attributed to the male.

Feeding and vaccinations of the pups are costly as well. You must give only good quality pup foods and at the same time, you should also make sure that the female regains her strength. Again, you need to go back often to the vet's clinic.

In most females, there is the possibility of ongoing health problems. Be on the look out for breast cancers and ovarian cancers because females who gave birth are more prone to such conditions.

Have you tried computing the costs of dog breeding? If you're going to do it for business, the income you might earn may not be enough to cover the expenses not unless you're going on large-scale breeding. However, if you're going to breed for personal reasons, it's a rewarding activity.

Guide to Responsible Dog Breeding

Prepare Yourself for Breeding a Litter

Breeding dogs has been a passion for people through many centuries. Part art, part science, and total devotion, breeding will show you all the best in the human-and-dog bond. It is exciting and challenging.

Breeding purebred dogs is also time consuming, expensive, and, occasionally, heartbreaking. If you go forward, your underlying purpose should be to improve the breed — not just increase its numbers.

Breeding a litter should begin with knowledge. Responsible breeders devote time to learning as much as they can about their breed, about canine health and training, and about AKC rules. How can you become an expert?

Study your breed standard. This is the official version of the "perfect" breed specimen and should be the starting place for any breeder. The AKC offers breed videos with real-life examples, and many parent clubs offer more detailed, illustrated versions of their standards for more in-depth research.

Attend dog events. Watch dogs in action and study the pedigrees of those you like. Ask questions of breeders involved in your breed.

Breed to Improve

The motto of the responsible breeder of purebred dogs is "Breed to Improve."

Every dog is the best dog in the world to its owner. Responsible breeders, however, know to avoid "kennel blindness" — in other words, they take a step back and honestly evaluate the good and bad points of their dogs before making the decision to breed. The goal of breeding, after all, is to produce a better dog and a quality pet.

Examine your dog carefully. Recognize its flaws. If you decide to continue with the breeding process, look for a mate that will eliminate or balance those flaws.

One of the best ways to get an objective opinion of your dog is to test it against others. Consider attending a dog show to determine how your dog measures up against the best specimens of its breed.

Understand the Commitment

Raising puppies is a full-time job. During the first couple of weeks the dam normally takes care of the puppies' needs, but complications, such as a dam with no milk or an orphaned litter, may arise. It is the breeder's responsibility to provide a safe, warm, dry place for the puppies and proper food and water for the bitch.

Puppies are even more work (and more fun!) when they are weaned. The extra feeding, cleanup, grooming, training, and veterinary care adds up to a lot of hours — and not much free time for you.

Another factor that you must consider is the financial cost of having a litter of puppies. From the genetic screening and health tests before breeding to the extra food, supplies, and medical care required after the puppies are born, the cost of whelping and raising puppies can be very high, especially if complications arise.

Responsible breeders make sure that their puppy goes to an owner who will provide it with the same love and devotion for life that the breeder has provided. This means careful screening and evaluation of each person or family interested in getting a puppy.

Responsible breeders learn everything they can about their breed and know all the pros and cons of ownership. It is important to share this information — including the negative aspects — with prospective puppy owners. You should be ready to explain why a dog requiring a lot of coat care or training may not be the best match for a workaholic or why a tiny dog may not be appropriate for a family with small, active children. You should be committed to placing puppies with owners who will provide excellent care.

Choose A Suitable Mate

When selecting a breeding partner (most likely a sire for your dam), there is a simple principle to bear in mind: mate animals that complement one another. Choose a dog whose bloodlines will strengthen your bitch's weaknesses and emphasize her good qualities. For example, if your bitch's coat is not as good as it might be, then find a partner with a good coat, from a line of dogs with good coats. Of course, practicing this common sense maxim can be very complex because you must weigh all the factors that contribute to the dogs' traits and appearances. This is an area where research and the advice and experience of other breeders are invaluable.

Two vital factors to keep in mind as you make your selection are temperament and health.

Temperament is a hereditary trait in dogs, although it can be influenced by other external factors. Selection over many generations eventually produced breeds with the correct temperament to pull sleds, follow scent on trails, or retrieve game. The inheritance factors of temperament are complex. However, you should never consider breeding a dog with a questionable temperament.

As far as health goes, you should be aware that dogs are subject to many hereditary defects, some of which are potentially crippling or fatal. If you breed, your goal should be to produce dogs that are not affected by the major known hereditary diseases occurring in your breed.

Know Your Genetics

To be an effective breeder, you should have a basic understanding of the science of genetics. Everything about your prospective puppies' health, soundness, looks, and temperament will be determined by the genes passed on by their parents, and by their parents before them. Therefore, the selection of a mating pair should not be made solely on the basis of the dog's or bitch's looks (or temperament or soundness, etc.), but should be based on an understanding of how the animal's genes contributed to its looks and of how those genes are passed on and expressed. That is why it is essential to study the pedigrees of your mating pair. The more knowledge you have as you make your selection, the more likely you are to produce a litter with the qualities you desire.

You should also be well-versed in the genetic problems that affect your breed. Genetic defects can occur in any breed and can affect any system in the body. Some genetic diseases may occur in many breeds; others occur in only one or a few breeds. The following is a brief explanation of how genetic defects may be inherited and expressed.

Diseases that follow a dominant pattern of inheritance need only one abnormal gene. That is, if only one parent is affected, the condition will show up in each successive generation. Some individuals may be only mildly affected with the condition, making it difficult to detect. In such cases, the condition can mistakenly be thought to skip generations.

Diseases that follow a recessive pattern of inheritance occur in homozygous individuals, meaning dogs with two abnormal genes. Dogs with one mutant and one normal gene are heterozygous, and they are carriers of the condition. They appear normal but can pass the abnormal gene to their offspring. Recessive mutant genes can be passed through many generations before emerging in the offspring of two dogs that carry the same genetic mutation.

Polygenic disorders result from the cumulative action of a number of different genes. The exact number of genes involved and their individual functions are difficult to determine, and the pattern of inheritance tends to vary from family to family. Polygenic inheritance can sometimes mimic either dominant or recessive inheritance, and this feature may lead to erroneous conclusions regarding the type of underlying genetic abnormality.

Chromosomal anomalies — defects in chromosome number and structure — can also cause genetic diseases. Dogs normally have 39 pairs of chromosomes on which genes are located. Major abnormalities in chromosome number and structure can produce serious defects.

Finalize Stud Contract

You have performed all necessary health checks, genetic screenings, and selected the perfect mate for your bitch. Now it's time to work out the details of the mating.

It is an excellent idea to work out a contract with the owner of the stud dog before breeding takes place. The agreement concerning stud fees should be in writing and clearly state all obligations and circumstances. The contract should be signed by all parties to the transaction, and each signer should receive a copy.

The stud fee is set by the stud dog's owner. The mode of payment may differ. The stud owner may request a cash fee, "pick of the litter," one or more puppies from the resulting litter, etc. The collection of the stud fee is the stud owner's responsibility. The contract may state that the owner of the sire is not obligated to sign an AKC litter registration application until the stud fee has been paid. Keep in mind that the AKC cannot settle disputes between individuals in regards to contracts and breeding arrangements.

Perform Pre-Breeding Health Checks

Good puppies start long before breeding ever takes place. Both parents need long-term care — what dog people call conditioning — to produce the best offspring. This means regular veterinary care, screening for genetic problems, pre-breeding tests, and regular exercise and good nutrition. Bitches should not be overweight and should have good muscle tone before breeding. Additionally, a bitch that is in good mental condition will make a better mother than a bitch that is insecure, snappy, or has an otherwise unstable temperament.

One month before breeding, the bitch should have a thorough pre-breeding physical examination by a veterinarian. Her vaccinations should be current, and she should be tested and treated for parasites.

You may also want to have the bitch and male tested for brucellosis, an infectious bacterial disease that can cause sterility or spontaneous abortion in affected dogs.

The age at which dogs reach sexual maturity depends to a large extent on their breed. Small breeds tend to mature faster than large breeds. On average, however, males become fertile after six months of age and reach full sexual maturity by 12 to 15 months. Healthy stud dogs may remain sexually active and fertile to old age. Adult males are able to mate at any time.

Bitches have their first estrus (also know as season or heat) after six months of age, although it can occur as late as 18 months to two years of age. Estrus recurs at intervals of approximately six months until late in life. During estrus, the female is fertile and will accept a male. The bitch should not be bred during her first season.

The bitch's cycle is divided into four periods.

Proestrus: The bitch attracts males, has a bloody vaginal discharge, and her vulva is swollen. Proestrus lasts approximately nine days; the bitch, however, will not allow breeding at this time.

Estrus: During this period, which also lasts approximately nine days, the bitch will accept the male and is fertile. Ovulation usually occurs in the first 48 hours; however, this can vary greatly.

Diestrus: Lasting 60 to 90 days, diestrus is the period when the reproductive tract is under the control of the hormone progesterone. This occurs whether or not the bitch becomes pregnant. False pregnancy, a condition in which the bitch shows symptoms of being pregnant although she has not conceived, is occasionally seen during diestrus.

Anestrus: No sexual activity takes place. Anestrus lasts between three and four months.

Keep in mind that AKC Rules do not allow, except with special documentation, the registration of a litter out of a dam less than 8 months or more than 12 years of age at the time of mating, or by a sire less than 7 months or more than 12 years of age at the time of mating.

MATING

Natural Breeding

Responsible breeders generally do not breed a bitch at the first heat to avoid imposing the stress of pregnancy and lactation on a young, growing animal. It is also customary to avoid breeding a bitch on consecutive heats to allow sufficient time for recuperation between pregnancies.

Most dogs are first bred between the 10th and 14th day after the onset of proestrus. As long as the bitch will accept the male, mating every other day for a total of two or three matings is generally considered sufficient. However, signs of proestrus are not obvious in some bitches. To catch the peak fertile period, a veterinarian may need to perform hormone tests or examine vaginal smears under a microscope.

Bitches are usually less inhibited by new environments so they are usually taken to the stud. Breedings involving young males proceed more smoothly if they are paired with experienced bitches. Sometimes human handlers must step in with assistance or guidance during breedings. Some breeds are more apt to need assistance than others because of anatomical considerations. Discussing this process with your own breeder will help you be prepared .

During breeding, the male mounts the female from the rear and clasps her midsection with his front legs. Rapid pelvic thrusts follow until penetration and ejaculation take place. After the pelvic thrusts cease, the dog and bitch will not separate for 10 to 30 minutes. Known as a tie, this results from a swollen section of the penis called the bulbus glandis. During the tie, the male may move around until he and the bitch are positioned rear to rear. Do not try to separate the dogs during the tie because it can injure either or both animals. After some time, they will part naturally.

Artificial Insemination

An artificial breeding may be carried out whenever a natural breeding is either impossible or undesirable. A vet collects sperm from a male and uses a syringe equipped with a catheter to deliver the sperm to the female's uterus. The catheter is threaded into the vulva while taking care to avoid the bladder. The sperm is then slowly expelled, and the bitch is kept quiet for about an hour to help ensure the sperm reach their destination. If all goes well, fertilization will take place and a litter will develop.

Pregnancy and Whelping Preparation

Watch for Signs of Pregnancy

Canine gestation lasts approximately 63 days. Signs of pregnancy include an increase in appetite, weight, and nipple size. However, a bitch with false pregnancy may also show these signs. A veterinarian can usually confirm a pregnancy through abdominal palpation at 28 days or by using ultrasound or X-rays. Once pregnancy is confirmed, you should talk to your vet about special feeding requirements and about what to expect during pregnancy, labor, and after birth. You should also be briefed on how to recognize and respond to an emergency.

Provide Proper Nutrition for your Pregnant Bitch

A bitch in good condition should continue into pregnancy with the same caloric intake that she had during adult maintenance. Her food intake should be increased only as her body weight increases, beginning about the last five weeks before whelping. Daily food intake should be increased gradually, so that at the time of whelping she may be eating 35 to 50 percent more than usual. As her weight and food intake increase, begin offering small, frequent meals to spare her the discomfort that larger meals can cause, especially in a small dog. If you have been feeding your bitch a well-balanced, high-quality diet, you should not need to add anything to her food during her pregnancy. However, some breeders advocate supplementation with a protein source such as evaporated milk, eggs, meat, or liver. These supplements should never represent more than 10 percent of the bitch's daily food intake.

Accustom your Bitch to the Whelping Box

It is a good idea to build a whelping box well in advance so the bitch has time to become accustomed to it. Unless you have already accustomed her to a whelping box, she may choose your closet or another inappropriate place for a delivery room.

An ideal whelping environment is warm, dry, quiet, draft-free, and away from all other dogs when possible. Confinement and whelping location of your bitch is relative to her breed and size.

A good whelping box is roomy and has low sides so you can easily reach in. It should also have a small shelf or roll bars running halfway up along the sides so the pups have something to crawl under to avoid getting rolled on by the bitch. Many breeders prefer to line the box with newspapers until after delivery because paper can be changed quickly when it becomes soiled. After whelping, newspapers are typically replaced with non-skid bath mats, outdoor carpeting, or something else that provides better footing for the puppies.

Be Alert for Signs of Labor

A few days before the bitch is ready to give birth, she may stop eating and start building a "nest" where she plans to have her puppies — if introduced properly, this should be in the whelping box you have prepared for her.

Shortly before whelping, the bitch's body temperature will drop to 99 degrees or lower (from a normal temperature of 100 to 102.5).

Approximately 24 hours after her temperature drops, she can be expected to enter the first stage of labor when the cervix dilates and opens the birth canal for the passage of puppies. At this time, she will pant, strain, and appear restless. This stage of labor is followed by actual abdominal straining and production of the puppies and placentas.

You should have on hand your veterinarian's phone number and the local emergency clinic.

Puppies Are Born

Most bitches give birth easily without the need of human help. Each puppy emerges in its own placental membrane, or sac, which must be removed before the puppy can breathe. The mother usually takes care of this by tearing off (and sometimes eating) the membrane and then severs the umbilical cord. After delivery, she will lick each puppy to stimulate its breathing.

You should keep track of how many placentas are delivered and ensure that the number matches the number of puppies because a retained placenta may cause problems.

You must take over if the bitch neglects to remove a sac or sever an umbilical cord. A puppy can remain inside the sac for only a few minutes before the oxygen supply is depleted. The sac membrane should be torn near the puppy's head and peeled backward until the puppy can be gently removed. Then you should remove mucus or fluids from the puppy's mouth and nose and gently rub the puppy with a towel to stimulate circulation. The umbilical cord can be tied with unwaxed dental floss and cut on the far side of the tie/knot about two inches from the abdomen. The cut end should be painted with iodine to prevent infection.

At the time of birth, the bitch will be busy cleaning her puppies, warming them, and allowing them to suckle. It is very important for the puppies to suckle soon after emerging from the womb. Suckling lets them ingest colostrum, a milk-like substance containing maternal antibodies which is produced in the mammary glands just after birth. Colostrum helps the newborn puppies fight infection in their early days while their own immune systems mature.

To track nourishment of the puppies, it is advisable to identify and weigh puppies during the first 2 weeks.

Consult Your Veterinarian if Complications Arise

If something goes wrong, don't hesitate to call your veterinarian for assistance. Signs of potential trouble include:

- Indications of extreme pain

- Strong contractions lasting for more than 45 minutes without delivery of a pup
- More than two hours elapsing between puppies with or without contractions
- Trembling, shivering, or collapse
- Passing a dark green or bloody fluid before the birth of the first puppy (after the first puppy, this is normal)
- No signs of labor by the 64th day after her last mating

Keep Your Puppies Warm, Fed and Clean

Temperature

A newborn puppy cannot control its body temperature and must be kept in a warm environment. Chilling will stress the puppy and predispose it to infectious disease; overheating can kill it. The environmental temperature can be controlled with a well-insulated electric heating pad or a heat lamp. But make sure the puppies have a cooler place to crawl to if they become too warm.

The immediate environmental temperature should be kept between 85 and 90 degrees for the first five days of life. From the seventh to the tenth day, the temperature can be gradually reduced to 80 degrees; by the end of the fourth week it can be brought down to 75 degrees.

Nursing

The first milk produced by the bitch after whelping is called colostrum. Every puppy needs to ingest colostrum as early as possible after birth and certainly during the first 24 hours of life. Colostrum contains a number of substances that are beneficial to the puppy, including immunoglobulins that protect newborns from the infectious diseases to which the mother is immune.

For your nursing bitches, one thing to keep a look out for is canine mastitis. It is not that common, but you should be aware of it. Canine mastitis is a breast infection in bitches, usually occurring a few weeks after whelping. Normally, the breasts of a lactating bitch are warm and enlarged. If the breasts seem to be red, dark, hot, or painful when touched, then you should contact your vet immediately. Advanced canine mastitis presents itself as a hard, hot and almost black breast segment, which is extremely painful for the bitch when touched. Canine mastitis can be caused by weaning puppies too early, severe scratches from puppies' claws, or some other infection. A bitch with canine mastitis may be running a fever, be listless, and may not eat. She also may not allow her puppies to nurse, and if she does, she will be "snappy" when they touch the affected area.

Caring for your bitch after whelping

Some bitches eat very little for the first day or two after whelping. Then their appetite and need for all nutrients rises sharply and peaks in about three weeks. During this entire period, adequate calcium, phosphorous, and vitamin D must be fed to avoid the onset of eclampsia. Optimal amounts of these nutrients are already present in a high-quality diet so further supplementation is unnecessary. Eclampsia causes nervousness, whimpering, unsteady gait, and spasms. Although very serious, it is readily cured by prompt veterinary treatment.

After whelping, the bitch ideally should be about the same weight as when she was bred, but not more than 5 to 10 percent heavier. For three weeks after whelping, she will need two or three times more food than her normal maintenance diet to help her provide nourishing milk to her puppies. This food should be divided into three or four meals. The composition of the food should be the same as it was during the last third of her pregnancy; only the amount per day should change.

Care for Orphaned Puppies

Newborn puppies must be hand fed if their mother is either unable or unwilling to nurse them. Cow's milk is a poor substitute for bitch's milk, which is more concentrated and has twice the level of protein, almost double the calories, and more than twice the calcium and phosphorous content. For feeding puppies, a commercial puppy formula is recommended; carefully follow the manufacturer's instructions.

Remember that puppies grow very rapidly so make sure you weigh them every day before you calculate how much to feed them.

You may need to start with slightly less formula at each feeding and gradually increase the amount as the puppy responds favorably to hand feeding. Steady weight gain and well-formed feces are the best evidence of satisfactory progress. If diarrhea develops, immediately reduce the puppy's intake to half the amount previously fed, then gradually increase it again to the recommended level. Diarrhea in newborns can be very dangerous so consult a veterinarian for advice.

Never prepare more formula than is required for any one day because milk is a medium for bacterial growth. Maintain sanitary conditions at all times. Before feeding, warm the formula to about 100 degrees or near body temperature. Using a bottle and nipple, hold the bottle at an angle to prevent air bubbles. The hole in the nipple can be enlarged slightly with a hot needle to let the milk ooze out slowly when the bottle is inverted. The puppy should suck vigorously, but should not nurse too rapidly. Consult a veterinarian if the puppies are not nursing well. You may need to resort to tube feeding, which is best taught by a health professional.

Newborn puppies must be stimulated to defecate and urinate after each feeding. Ordinarily the mother's licking provides this stimulation, but orphaned puppies will need human intervention. Gently massage the puppy's anal region with a cotton ball that has been dipped in warm water.

Gentle body massage is also beneficial for any hand-reared puppy. Massage stimulates the circulation and thoroughly awakens the puppy. Stroke the puppy's sides and back with a soft cloth. The best time for a massage seems to be when the puppies are waking up and you're waiting for the formula to get warm.

Wean Puppies from Their Mother

There are many rules of thought about weaning your puppies. Experienced breeders tend to use methods that work best for them and their respective breed. It is recommended that you contact your veterinarian to discuss a feeding regimen for your litter.

Most puppies begin the weaning process at about two to four weeks of age. Some breeders recommend starting them off by offering a pan of puppy formula in place of their mother's milk. Other breeders combine the puppy formula with some presoaked or grinded dry puppy food and/or baby rice cereal to create gruel.

As the puppies get older, most breeders start adding more food and decrease the amount of formula.

To avoid digestive upsets, be sure to introduce all changes in food or feeding schedules gradually.

Sending Your Pups to Their New Homes

By this time you have learned everything you can about your breed, and you know all the pros and cons of ownership. It's important to share this information — including the negative aspects — with prospective puppy owners. You should be ready to explain why a dog requiring a lot of coat care or training may not be the best match for a workaholic, or why a tiny dog may not be appropriate for a family with small, active children.

A responsible breeder makes sure that their puppies go to good homes. This means careful screening and evaluation of each person or family interested in getting a puppy. Knowing the right questions to ask prospective owners helps breeders get a feel for the type of home they will provide. Some of these questions can include:

Why does the person or family want a dog? Why has the person or family chosen this particular breed?

Who will be primarily responsible for the dog's care?

Do you have the time to meet the demanding needs of the puppy/dog? Time for feeding, training and exercise?

Are there any children? If so, how old are they? How would they be instructed in the care of the dog?

Does anyone in the household have allergies?

Are the new owners committed to the grooming and health maintenance?

What is the potential owner's attitude toward training and obedience?

How often is someone at home?

Will they have time to walk and play with the dog?

This means applying for litter registration in plenty of time to supply applications to owners at the time of sale. You should explain the benefits of registration to the owners and help them complete the registration application. Conditions such as limited registration or co-ownership should be explained in full. You will also want to provide the new puppy owners with vaccination/health records, feeding instructions, health guarantees, return policy, any health or genetic tests, as well as a copy of the sales agreement/contract.

Commit Yourself to the Puppies for Life

For breeders, responsibility doesn't end when their puppies leave with new owners. Responsible breeders make sure their puppies' new families know they can turn to them with any questions or problems that arise throughout the puppies' lives.

As a breeder, you will be gratified by phone calls and letters describing your puppies' first teeth, birthday parties, and other milestones. You'll be thrilled to receive photos of a puppy's first show win or portraits with the puppy right in the middle of a happy family. But you will also have to be ready for bad news: a family splitting up and leaving the dog homeless; a vet contacting you about an unforeseen hereditary illness; a dog you thought would be a great obedience prospect biting a young child. As a breeder, you will need to be there with advice and support for all these situations. Responsible breeders answer questions, provide resources, and assist with problems that may come up. Responsible breeders assist in re-homing or take in puppies should the need arise.

Encourage New Owners to Register Their Puppy

Getting All Your Puppies Registered!

Before you send your puppies to their new homes, be sure to

inform new owners of their best source (besides yourself!) for information on sharing a long, fulfilling, active life with their new pet.

Glossary of Dog Breeding and Pregnancy Terms

There are quite a few terms you'll hear in the course of any discussion on dog breeding. This list of common terms and definitions provides important dog breeding information that will help any beginner better understand the entire process.

Bitch - This the correct term for a female dog.

Dam - This is the designation given to the mother of a litter.

Stud - The stud is the male dog that performs the breeding on the bitch.

Sire - This is the designation given to the father of the litter.

Litter - This term applies to a group of puppies that are born from the same pregnancy.

Heat cycle - This is the active period of a bitch's reproductive cycle. It's characterized by a bloody discharge, the release of eggs for fertilization and a period of active willingness to breed.

Ovaries - These are reproductive organs that release ovum for fertilization during a bitch's heat cycle.

Eggs - This is the common term for reproductive cells that are created when ovum are released from the ovaries and are fertilized by sperm. A fertilized egg is known as a zygote and develops into an embryo once it implants in the uterine wall.

Sperm - These are minute organisms produced by the male

that fertilize the bitch's eggs and deliver the stud's DNA.

Vulva - This is the opening to the bitch's reproductive tract. The vulva swells considerably at the beginning of the heat cycle and then softens to facilitate breeding.

Penis and testicles - These are the stud's reproductive organs designed to produce and deliver sperm.

Gestation - This term applies to the entire period of pregnancy.

Whelp - This is a term used to describe a newborn pup.

Whelping - This is the act of giving birth, and it is also simply known as "labor."

Whelping box - This is a prepared box in which the bitch gives birth. You can purchase a commercial whelping box, or you can create one yourself from a cardboard box, a small children's pool or by using blueprints to build one from wood.

Contractions - These are spasms of the uterus that are designed to propel the pup along the birth canal toward delivery.

Water bag - This is the thin yet durable membrane or "birth sac" that surrounds each puppy in utero. Nearly all pups are born in this protective sac which must be broken immediately after the pup is born or it will suffocate.

Umbilical cord - This is the fleshy cord that is attached between a pup's abdomen and the placenta. It must be severed after the pups' birth either by the mother chewing the cord or by cutting it with sterilized scissors.

Uterus - This is organ wherein the embryos attach and grow throughout the pregnancy.

Placenta - This is the organ that attaches each embryo to the uterine wall. It supports each pup's growth and development by delivering oxygen and nutrients, and also by carrying waste away via the umbilical cord. When a puppy is born, its umbilical cord is still attached to the placenta. The placenta may be delivered with the pup, or it may take a few minutes longer to be delivered with the next contraction.

Line breeding - This term refers to a planned breeding between family members used to secure desirable qualities in the progeny. Line breedings include breedings between grandparent/ grandchild, uncle/niece, aunt/nephew half-brother/half-sister and breedings with relatives even further apart.

Inbreeding - These are breedings between closely related individuals including mother/son, father/daughter and full-brother/full-sister. Such breedings are typically undesirable and may produce congenital defects in the pups.

Outcrossing - A breeding between two non-related dogs.

Tie - This term is used to describe the swelling near the base of the dog's penis that temporarily binds the dog to the bitch during intercourse. As the swelling develops, the bitch's muscles clamp down around it to hold the organ in place. This helps to ensure proper delivery of semen, and though not completely necessary for producing a litter, it does increase the chance for fertilization.

Dog Breeding How To's

These are just the basics of what's involved with breeding a dog. Other topics you should spend time learning about are:

Understanding canine genetics and breeding to find the best pairing to further the development of your breed. You should learn as well about the myriad of health tests recommended for both the stud and bitch before deciding to breed.

While a female dog can go into heat at the age of six months, a responsible breeder will not breed before a female dog reaches maturity which is between 12 and 24 months depending on size. Male dogs can be bred up to any age, even as seniors, although their mobility may prevent them from breeding the older they get. Under the AKC, a stud cannot be older than 12 years and a dam must be at least eight months.

Know the signs and symptoms involved with a female going into heat, what to expect during pregnancy and even recognizing a false pregnancy. You'll also need to recognize the signs your dog is ready to give birth.

Whelping puppies including how the proper supplies you'll need to keep the mom comfortable, including buying a whelping box or building one.

What to do once the puppies are born and helping the mother to come through the process healthy and comfortable.

Preventing disease including the deadly parvo and properly vaccinating your puppies. Understanding proper socialization for the puppies as well is critical to their future behavioral health.

Finding the best homes for the puppies, including interviewing the prospective buyers and preparing a solid contract.

How Often Do Dogs Go Into Heat?

Bitches should have an obvious heat cycle by 24 months of age. Although bitches vary in the frequency of their heat cycles, an average female goes through heat about every seven months. A bitch is not considered abnormal unless she has not had an obvious heat cycle for one year.

Is It Okay to Breed a Bitch in Back-to-Back Heat Seasons?

That depends on how many puppies she whelped the first season and how well she maintained her body condition during pregnancy, whelping, and lactation. If she had several puppies and was thin by the time they were weaned, she probably cannot regain normal body condition before she is in heat again and thus should not be bred. If she had few puppies at the first breeding and is in excellent body condition, she potentially could be bred again. Every circumstance and every bitch should be evaluated individually.

What Do You Feed a Pregnant Dog?

A growth or performance food, like Purina® Pro Plan® SPORT 30/20, is best to feed a pregnant bitch because they are nutrient dense and thus require less food to sustain her increasing energy needs. Particularly later in the pregnancy when her uterus takes up much of the space of the abdomen, she may have trouble eating a significant amount of food. At whelping, a bitch should weigh 5-to-10 percent more than before breeding. Try to avoid obesity as it is associated with difficulty whelping, increased birth defects in neonates, and stillbirths. Likewise, a thin body condition can cause conception failure, loss of pregnancy, and low-weight pups.

How Soon Should Puppies Nurse After Birth?

Puppies cannot make their own antibodies at birth, so it is important that they receive their dam's first milk, colostrum, which is rich in disease-protecting antibodies. Puppies can absorb these antibodies from their intestinal tract for only about the first 24 hours of life. Don't be concerned if your bitch does not nurse until all the puppies are born. This is common behavior that generally causes no risk to puppies.

What Causes Small Litters?

The most likely culprit is breeding at the wrong time. The optimal breeding day for litter size is two days post-ovulation, as determined by your veterinarian based on progesterone measurements. Other possible causes of small litters are hypothyroidism, uterine infection, and advanced age of the bitch.

Was the Runt Conceived Later Than His Littermates?

Probably not. Runt puppies most likely are the same age as their littermates but had poor placentation. Bitches release all their eggs over a 24-hour span. Even if the conception of that small pup occurred later than conception of the other puppies, all pups float around free for 17 days before implantation and formation of the placenta.

DOG BREEDING – HOW TO FIND A DOG MATE

If you have a female pet dog, you might be thinking of breeding her in the near future. You can't really tell how long your dog will live and if she has puppies, there will be instant replacements. Training puppies may seem hard but it can be a very rewarding task. You can even sell the other puppies if you like especially if there are too many of them already. Being a dog breeder is not simple and if you're plotting to be involved in dog breeding, you should find the aptly dog.

As a breeder, it will be your dependability to take care of the puppies after birth. At some point, you will be attached to the puppies but you shouldn't let emotions hinder your plans. You must prepare yourself because you need to let go of the puppies sooner or later.

Handling new born puppies may seem a tough job but you must first look for the aptly mate for your dog. You can breed your dog when she is already two being or even older. You see, breeding very childish dogs may not be a very excellent thought because the mother dog may not be responsible enough to care for the puppies. When you finally start breeding, you must also see to it that you're dog gets the aptly shots at the aptly time. Try to schedule an appointment with the vet so that you can easily choose the perfect partner for breeding. So, can you handle the tasks involved in breeding dogs? If you can, why don't you start looking for a dog mate?

Finding a dog mate can be very tough. It will often depend on the particular dog that you have. Well loved dog breeds are simple to find. If you can afford to pay for an advertisement on your local paper, you may do so because this is an brilliant way to let other people know that you're breeding dogs. Don't forget to check out dog breeding websites because you might be able to find helpful information there too. Another option is through word-of-mouth. Start by informing your family, friends, and relatives that you're looking for a dog mate.

By putting all these things at work, someone will know about it. When you finally find a dog mate, you should talk to its owner. Contact the owner and set up a meeting. Question for the breeding charges or fees. That way, you can immediately determine if the price is reasonable. If you can't afford the fees, you can still search for other owners of possible dog mates for your dog.

There are those who set a standard fee for dog breeding and when the puppies are bon, they will be privileged to pick one of the pups. Taking care of puppies is really fun and exciting. Don't get too attached though; that way, when it's time for the pups to leave, you won't get hurt.

Start breeding your female dog now. Choose among the options available so that you can easily find the owner of a possible dog mate for your dog. By investing some of your time, you can gain a lot of money once you sell your pups. Dog breeding is a profitable business and if you can penetrate the market. Pick the best dog breed which is saleable.

DOG BREEDING – THINGS TO THINK ABOUT

Some dog owners extend their love for animals into an interest in breeding their dog. Breeding is more of a responsibility than a passing interest, and as such, there are a few things to consider before immersing yourself and your dog in the process. This short checklist identifies some helpful pointers which will increase the odds of a successful breeding experience.

Consider your dog's age, breed, and health status. To begin with, veterinarians recommend not breeding dogs that are less than eighteen months old. This allows you as an owner the opportunity to schedule tests that rule out any genetic defects or conditions they could pass on to their offspring. It also makes sure that your female is physically mature enough to carry a litter of puppies.

There are also health issues which can affect your decision to breed your dog. These health concerns can be general, as in the case of brucellosis (a bacterial infection spread among breeding dogs that can contribute to infertility, abortion, or stillborn puppies), or a male dog may simply not be fertile.

Alternatively, they can be specific to certain breeds. Dachshunds and Basset Hounds have long spines and short legs, for instance, making them prone to back problems as they age. Retrievers, Shepherds, and Great Danes frequently develop hip dysplasia, easily confirmed by x-rays. Collies are predisposed to two eye disorders, Collie Eye Anomaly and Progressive Retinal Atrophy. Testing your dog before breeding will let you know if he is carrying any of these conditions. If he is, then he's not a good candidate for parenthood.

Regular treatment for heartworm, intestinal worms and fleas, as well as standard vaccinations to protect against the most common viruses (parvovirus, parainfluenza, distemper, hepatitis, and leptospirosis) are essential to keep your animal in good health for breeding. In addition, good nutrition and regular exercise are important in increasing the chances of producing healthy puppies.Pay a visit to your veterinarian to make sure there aren't any potential problems that need to be addressed before deciding to breed your dog.

Finally, you should carefully consider the reasons behind your decision to breed a dog. If money from the sale of purebred puppies is the sole source of inspiration, consider the expenses involved from beginning to end. Stud fees, genetic testing, veterinary care, a possible cesarean delivery, and the cost of feeding, worming, and vaccinating puppies will quickly eat into any profits you may earn. Unless you've spent considerable time and effort researching such a venture, you must be prepared for these costs, and be prepared to make a financial loss from a litter.

Another poor reason for breeding is to obtain a dog just like the one you already have. This isn't likely to happen, because your pups are just as likely to resemble the other parent, or have characteristics that are a mixture of both parents.

A more sensible approach to dog breeding relies on selecting characteristics that you hope to pass on to future generations of the breed. Each breeding should be carefully planned to result in puppies that are an improvement on the generation before. This is how dog breeds are continually improved.

Breeding dogs is a rewarding pastime, but make sure your motives are honorable, and you have the health and well being of your dog and its breed foremost in your mind.

THREE REASONS WHY YOU SHOULD NOT BREED YOUR DOG!

We all think our dog is the most beautiful in the world, and they would have beautiful babies. It's true. But, on its own that's no reason to breed them. Let's look at some reasons why breeding your dog might not be the right thing for you.

You shouldn't breed your dog unless you are prepared to do any necessary genetic testing to make sure you don't produce pups with hereditary diseases. You can find out what testing your dog needs by researching your breed online, asking at your local breed club or checking your Kennel Club site.

You shouldn't breed your dog unless you have budgeted for expected and unexpected expenses, and you have the time to do the job properly. Puppies will need vaccinating and worming, and a big litter will eat a lot! They're the expected expenses. What will you do if your dog needs a caesarian in the middle of the night? Make sure you have the funds to cover any eventuality. Now the time. Some dogs aren't good mums, or they become unwell and can't feed their pups. Can you bottle feed a litter every few hours until they can eat on their own?

You shouldn't breed your dog unless you are prepared to care for each and every pup until they find the right forever home, and you are committed to taking that dog back if at any time their new owner can't keep them. You have created a life, you are responsible for it. Don't let your pups end up at animal shelters.

One of the worst reasons for breeding a dog that I have ever heard is so that the children can experience the miracle of birth. Honestly!! You can see that on YouTube and you don't produce a litter of pups that may or may not get a good home. Think about it, these are dogs' lives we are talking about.

DOG BREEDING AND HEREDITARY EYE PROBLEMS

When you're into dog breeding, you should be aware that there will always be potential hereditary problems. Although this is not true all the time, you should be on the look out for such problems because it can be passed on to the puppies. Keep on reading and you will find out what these hereditary problems are.

Firstly, you need to learn as much information as possible about the particular dog breed you're handling. Thorough screening is needed so that you can prevent additional problems in the future. Make sure that you also look into the bloodlines of your dogs. This is necessary to ensure the health and condition of the pups.

Eye problems are the most common dilemmas encountered by most dog breeders. These problems are:

1) PRA or Progressive Retinal Atrophy – if this problem is not addressed at an early stage, your

dog can suffer from total blindness. Some breeds are affected by PRA once they reach 2-3 years or before the breeding period. In some cases, dogs tend to suffer from PRA when they are already 4-8 years. If you're breeding Irish Setters, you're in luck because there is already a PRA test which is available to those who want to breed them. It is vital that breeders identify if their dog is a carrier of the eye problem. You see, late onset of PRA can affect breeding programs.

2) CEA or Collie Eye Anomaly – collie breeds can be affected by

this eye problem which can include the border, bearded, smooth, rough, and closely related breeds. The condition varies wherein some dogs are hardly affected but others get completely blind. This problem is hereditary. Even if the dogs you're breeding are not suffering from the CEA but serves as a carrier of the problem, it can produce a pup that is severely affected by CEA.

3) Retinal Dysplasia – eventual blindness is the result of retinal dysplasia. The problem can start as early as the puppy days of the dog but late onset of the problem can

make it hard to identify which dogs have it.

4) Entropion and Ectropion – try to look closely at the eyelids of your dog. This problem refers to the eyelids turning in (entropion) or out (ectropion). This eye problem can cause pain.

5) Cataracts – you need to identify if your dog has juvenile cataract; if this is the case, find another dog to breed. Cataracts have different causes and they are also in different forms.

Every year, dogs should be checked by a vet certified by the

AVCO. Visit the CERF or Canine Eye Registry Foundation if you live in the United States. Dogs registered under this foundation are free from any eye problems. It is vital for dogs to be checked annually to ensure that they are free from eye problems which are considered hereditary. There are times when the problems show up late but if you consult with CERF, you're guaranteed to breed to a dog without potential eye problems.

Dog breeding is serious business. Even if you're only doing it for pleasure or as a hobby, you should ensure that the puppies are in best condition. Who would want to purchase a pup with eye problems? It is your responsibility to make sure that the parents are not carriers of the eye problems or are not presently affected by it.

THE IMPORTANCE OF MEDICAL CHECKS

When breeding dogs, you need to have a stud and a bitch. Without them, you can't produce puppies. Since the two dogs will serve as your tool to have puppies, you need to have them regularly checked. Medical checks are extremely important to ensure the health and overall condition of your dogs.

If you want to become a full time breeder or you simply want to produce additional dogs for your family, you should know a great deal about dog breeding. If this is your first time, then you still have a lot to learn. You can't produce healthy puppies if there is sterility problems involved. If one or both parents have sterility problems, the puppies have very little chance of survival. They may be aborted or they can die later on. Are you aware that this condition can be transmitted to humans through feces or urine? This is true and as a dog breeder, you should be aware of it and not only that, you should also be extra careful when handling them.

The condition is called brucellosis and it can also be transmitted to other dogs through sexual intercourse or through secretions found in the kennels of the affected dog. Vaccinations are important to ensure that the male dog is in general good health and the female should have the capacity to withstand the rigors and stresses of pregnancy. Aside from brucellosis, you should also look out for other conditions that can compromise the health and safety of your dogs. Some dogs are deaf. Although it is hard to tell at first, with close observation, you may be able to identify this problem immediately.

Have your dog undergo BAER test and if your pet is truly deaf, you should have your dog neutered. Who says heart conditions are only for humans? Well, dogs can also suffer heart conditions. A very common example of a heart condition is the SAS or Subaortic

Stenosis. Other problems are caused by malformations of the valves or the heart itself. Other diseases to watch out for are Willebrand's disease, hemophilia, digestive problems, malabsorptive syndromes, epilepsy, allergies, and incorrect temperament. Dog breeding is not a very easy activity.

Whether you're doing it to earn extra income or just a simple past time, you should ensue the health of the stud and bitch, as well as their future puppies. Breeding involves a lot of research work. You should know a lot about the ancestors of your dog breeds. You can conduct an online research or you can read good books on dog breeding. If you can consult an expert breeder, you may do so because you can learn a lot from the pros. You can't get it all the first time but if you're in luck, a litter of healthy and cute puppies are guaranteed.

Learn everything and don't hesitate to exert a little effort. If you educate yourself, you will not find it hard to deal with dog problems. Medical checks and dog breeding go hand in hand. You can't possibly produce healthy puppies if you don't have good male and female dogs.

Find a local vet who can help you with the regular checkups of your precious pets. Now that you know the importance of regular checkups, make sure that you include it in your list of priorities.

Do you have the resources to breed successfully?

Breeding puppies successfully is time-consuming, potentially costly and requires quite a bit of knowledge. Before you begin, you should be clear that you have the resources to breed properly.

So what will you need?

1. Time

You need to be able to be able to give the dam all the care she needs through whelping and the first eight weeks of the puppies' lives, which is the earliest they can go to new homes.

You will need to keep an eye out for signs of infection in the mother, keep the whelping box clean and fresh, ensure the family has the vet checks they need and generally ensure a calm, quiet atmosphere while the pups are tiny.

If something goes wrong, for example the dam does not produce enough milk for the pups, the process can be even more time-consuming, as you will need to find a foster mother or use milk replacer products.

2. Money

You will need to be able to cover veterinary costs such as pre-breeding tests, vaccinations and attendance during the birth if whelping is not straightforward.

In a worst-case scenario, you may need to deliver the pups by caesarean section, or have the dam treated for issues such as haemorrhage or infection.

The best way to protect yourself and your pets against costly vet bills is to take out multi pet insurance. By combining all your pets on a single policy, you can save money and ensure you have the cover you need.

3. Knowledge

You will need to know how to support your dog through pregnancy and whelping, including understanding the signs that veterinary assistance is required. You should be familiar with all you need to do to keep the bitch and her litter healthy in the early days, and how to socialise the pups when they find their feet.

Choosing a stud

The stud you choose should have a pedigree that is compatible with your bitch, as well as a clean bill of health. Before breeding, the stud should be checked for inherited diseases which apply to that breed.

Of course, you can always choose to create a crossbreed litter. Some mixed breed dogs are immensely popular, mixing the best characteristics of two pedigrees.

Celebrated examples include the Cavachon (Cavalier King Charles Spaniel and Bichon Frise), the Labradoodle (Labrador Poodle), the Cockapoo (Cocker Spaniel and Poodle) and the Goberian (Golden Retriever and Siberian Husky).

While crossbreeding can be very successful, producing a unique-looking dog who often escapes congenital issues associated with the parents' breeds, it is also an unpredictable process.

The size and temperament of crossbreed dogs is hard to predict, and deliveries can also be higher risk, perhaps even requiring a caesarean section.

CONCLUSION

Dog breeding is emotionally hard and it will break your heart repeatedly. However, when doing it for the good reasons and not just for cosmetics and profits (extreme breeding) will allow your to keep on breeding healthier and better dogs, and that's very fulfilling.

Whether you are breeding boxers, papillons, labradors, american bullies or any other dog breed, just do your homework and know as much as possible before you even plan your first mating.

Dog breeding for beginners is a wonderful adventure that started now but will need you to persevere for several years. And you know when you should start breeding? When you don't think of yourself as a beginner.

Made in the USA
Monee, IL
24 August 2021